CW01574745

ELEANOR ROOSEVELT

Cover Image: Eleanor Roosevelt, 1898

Table of Contents

Introduction

In Riverside Park, Manhattan, New York, there stands a statue of Eleanor Roosevelt. Some say this was the first of its kind, honoring a First Lady of the United States. This woman is an American icon as a leader who changed the world for the better.

But, who is the real woman behind this iconic figure? Surely no one is perfect, even someone as humane and reasonable as Eleanor was during her time in the spotlight. The truth is that she did not fit the mold society gave her. This made her both remarkable and controversial in her time.

Today, people may see her as a mild-mannered do-gooder. If they do, they are missing the value of the legacy she left the world. In her time, she knocked down barriers of race and gender and promoted human rights through her words and her deeds. And, she did it in a way that no American woman had done before her.

She was not just a president's wife. She went beyond that role to build her own constituency and make a place for herself among some of the most powerful people in the world. She never sat idly by when she could work towards the betterment of human conditions. She accomplished a high level of personal power and prestige simply by doing what was right to her and speaking truth to the American people.

At the same time, Eleanor had a life full of friendship, passion, and influence. She was not always pleasant. She disagreed with her husband, Franklin, on many occasions. However, when the romance between them died, she continued to work with him as a teammate to help him achieve his political goals, all the while using the power of the White House for her own noble pursuits.

Eleanor Roosevelt is an ideal role model for women – indeed, for all people everywhere.

Chapter 1

Growing Up Granny

Anna Eleanor Roosevelt was an unusual child. Her mother unkindly called her "Granny" when she was a very young child because she had such a wise and old-fashioned demeanor. And, it was no wonder, considering the family she was born into. She, like many other children in her situation, may have adopted this way of being as a defensive response to a turbulent and unsteady environment. Whatever the impetus was, she used it to her full advantage as she made her way into the world.

That is not to say that she was poor – far from it. On October 11, 1884, Eleanor Roosevelt was born into a life of privilege and abundance. The family was wealthy and well-connected. Her father, Elliott Bulloch Roosevelt, and her mother, Anna Rebecca Hall, were socialites living in Manhattan, New York and moving in the most elite social circles. She was the niece of

President Theodore Roosevelt and tennis greats Edward Ludlow Hall and Gill Hall III.

Life was not easy for little Eleanor and her younger brothers, Elliot Jr. and Hall. Her father had an affair with the family servant and fathered the woman's child. He went away traveling for long periods, sometimes taking along his wife, sometimes not. His absence was disheartening for Eleanor because she idolized and adored her warm and carefree father. He was often ill and away for medical treatments. Although his doctors did not know what the problem was, many experts now believe he may have had epilepsy. Eleanor's mother was bitter. When she had terrible migraines, Eleanor soothed her.

Eleanor's life took an even sadder turn when her mother became ill with diphtheria and died. Eleanor was eight years old at that time. Her little brother, Elliot, Jr. died the next year. Her father, an alcoholic, died when she was not quite ten years old, and it was not a peaceful end. He jumped from a window during alcohol detox and died while having a seizure.

Eleanor was sent to live with her maternal grandmother, who took good care of her basic needs without offering her much affection.

However, Eleanor felt that as the older sibling, she should be a substitute mother for her younger surviving brother, Hall. She took care of him when he was a child and continued to watch over him from afar after he became an adult.

Eleanor was considered plain, and she felt sure that she was. Her mother had told her so, and now others joined in the chorus. The sadness of her childhood caused her to be prone to depression, then and throughout her life. Yet, she felt that as long as she was loyal, wise, and honest, she would have every opportunity for a good life.

When Eleanor was about five years old, a private tutor and his assistant began coming to her house to teach her math, English and several other languages. At the age of six, her mother placed her in a convent school. She was always a good student, but it was not until she was 14 and went away to Allenswood Girl's Academy in London that she got special attention. There, Marie Souvestre, the teacher who ran the school, took her under her wing.

In addition to learning the subjects taught to all at the school, Eleanor learned about geography, history, and philosophy under the private tutelage of Souvestre. The teacher even took her on trips to France and Italy, where they toured beyond the typical tourist locations to see what life was like for the working class. Souvestre, intent on shaking up the status quo, taught Eleanor to think critically and question authority.

Eleanor went back to her grandmother for her debut into New York society, but Eleanor would always look back fondly at the happy times she spent with Sovestre in London. Still, at this point, she was an adult and ready to take on real adult work for the first time.

Chapter 2

Eleanor and Franklin

For Eleanor Roosevelt, the single life was not for all about partying. She, like her parents, had many social connections and did spend time with them. However, that was not enough for her. She wanted to live a more meaningful life. Also, as an upper-class woman, she was expected to contribute to worthy social causes. This fit well with the ideas about social reform she had learned from Madame Souvestre.

She became interested in the Progressive movement championed by her uncle, Theodore. She met many of President Theodore Roosevelt's political friends and became a member of the National Consumers League. She also taught at a slum school as a volunteer for the Junior League of New York. She was, indeed, her own woman. But, then, something unexpected happened. She got involved with a man whose power and position would give her an even greater opportunity to do what she wanted most – to create change.

Eleanor had known Franklin Roosevelt casually most of her life. They were, after all, distant cousins and both traveled in the same social circles. On one occasion, Franklin asked Eleanor to dance, and the two had an enjoyable moment. Nothing ever came of it at that time, however.

Then, one day, when Eleanor was traveling by train to see her grandmother, Franklin saw her sitting there alone and was mesmerized. The two began seeing each other steadily after that. In November 1903, Franklin proposed marriage, but Franklin's mother, Sara, strongly disapproved. She took him on a long ocean cruise, hoping he would lose interest and the relationship would come to an end.

The opposite happened, though. Eleanor and Franklin became even more devoted to each other during their time apart. When he returned, he chose Colombia University over Harvard so he could be near her while he worked toward a law degree. On March 17, 1905, Eleanor, just 20 years old, married the 22-year-old Franklin. Theodore Roosevelt gave away the bride since her father was no longer living. The event made the front-page headline of the *New York Times*.

The young couple was in love, but Eleanor had a significant obstacle to overcome. Her mother-in-law, Sara, took charge of Eleanor and Franklin's new household. She chose their first home, along with all its furnishings, décor, and staff. She was always at Eleanor's side, telling her what choices to make and how to live her life. Eleanor began to become dependent on Sara and others. She accepted Sara's help but became ever more despondent as the time went on.

Chapter 3

A Mother, and Not

Eleanor Roosevelt once said she spent the better part of ten years either preparing for childbirth or recovering from it, and so had little time to do or think of anything else. This period of her life began before her daughter Anna was born in 1906. More children followed: James in 1907, Franklin Jr. in 1909, Elliot in 1910, Franklin Jr. in 1914, and John in 1916. The Roosevelt household was filled with the sounds of children, but these were not all happy times.

The first Franklin Jr. died less than a year after he was born. Eleanor and Franklin grieved the loss deeply. When Eleanor gave birth for the fifth time, they used the name again.

Eleanor loved her children immensely and wanted to give them a better childhood than she had had. However, her mother-in-law again intervened, telling her how to raise the children and care for their needs. Sara's presence loomed large in the household, and soon, the children were more attached to her than they were to their own mother. In fact, in later years, Sara would say that the children were more hers than Eleanor's.

As Sara took charge of her children, Eleanor spiraled further into dependence and depression. She had a breakdown at one point and realized that she had lost the individuality she once had. She was letting others – not just Sara, but anyone available – tell her how to behave. She was forming her opinions based on what others told her to think rather than thinking for herself as Madame Souvestre had taught her. It was a low point in her life.

However, Eleanor had come through many low points, and this was no exception. Eleanor continued to spend time with her children, reading to them, traveling with them, or enjoying family outings. However, at the same time, she began broadening her personal experience. She became active in social reform organizations again.

Furthermore, she began studying and learning about law and politics. FDR had finished college, worked as a lawyer, and made his way into the

State Senate of New York. Now, he was the U.S. Assistant Secretary of the Navy, pushing the government towards entering World War I.

Eleanor was busy, too. As the wife of a cabinet member, she had many social obligations. She was required to host and attend parties and teas with the wives of other cabinet members. Eleanor had more on her mind, however. Since Franklin's time in Albany as a state senator, she had been busy learning what was required to create change through legislation. She prepared herself again, but this time it was a birth of a different kind. This time she was birthing herself into the world of influence and power.

Chapter 4

Friendships and Romances

By the time FDR became assistant naval secretary, Eleanor knew the ins and out of being a politician's wife. She met her social duties as prescribed, even though she never liked the small talk that was a part of the job. She had a purpose now; she was determined to help FDR succeed in the political arena.

During World War I, Eleanor worked with the Navy Relief Society and the Red Cross. She and other notable Navy wives set up booths to feed members of the armed forces as they departed for Europe. After that, a Navy Chaplain approached her with a request for her assistance in providing emotional support for returning sailors.

She also took on the task of evaluating the sailors' problems and the state of the hospital where their mental health conditions were being treated. She convinced the Red Cross to set up a recreation center at the hospital and the Wilson administration to increase the hospital budget. She also went to the 1919 International Congress of Working Women and provided French translation services there. After the war, she toured battlefields with then-President Woodrow Wilson and his group.

In 1918, during FDR's stint as a junior cabinet member, Eleanor discovered that Franklin was involved in an extramarital romantic relationship. While unpacking from her husband's European trip, she found a cache of love letters from her personal secretary, Lucy Mercer, written to Franklin. She offered to divorce him, but he was well aware that his political aspirations would never be fulfilled if he agreed. The couple continued their marriage as a chaste partnership to further their social and political goals.

Eleanor moved away from intimate involvement with her husband and began spending more time and energy nurturing both personal and political relationships. These and other relationships blossomed then and throughout her life.

Franklin was the vice-presidential candidate in 1920, and Eleanor wanted to learn more so she could help him win. His press secretary and advisor, Louis Howe, struck up a friendship with her later on and spent a good deal of time showing her the ropes in the campaign process. He taught her how he reviewed and assessed speeches, how and when to release statements and other political strategies.

After losing his bid for the vice-presidential seat, FDR became governor of New York. Eleanor helped by establishing a social and political network of her own within the Democratic Party and among social reformers. She traveled with Caroline O'Day and Elinor Morgenthau, who become lifelong friends with Eleanor.

Later on, in the 1930s, Eleanor became good friends with Amelia Earhart. The two shared a playful relationship. Once, they slipped out of the White House to secretly go to a party. Another time, Amelia took Eleanor out for a plane ride. Amelia had planned to teach Eleanor how to fly, but there were two problems with that. First, Franklin was opposed to it. Second, Amelia and her plane were lost before they had the opportunity to do it. When Amelia's plane was lost, Eleanor pulled strings to facilitate the search for her.

When Franklin was running for president, Eleanor met AP reporter Lorena Hickok. Lorena, or Hick as Eleanor called her, was taking information to write a biography of Eleanor. Eleanor developed an ongoing relationship with her, writing long letters to her every day. The content of those letters suggests that the relationship was romantic, and maybe even sexual. Since Hick was a known lesbian, there is speculation about whether they had an affair. J. Edgar Hoover, FBI director at the time, kept up an investigation of Eleanor during the time she was the First Lady and may have had evidence about this subject. Scholars disagree about the type of relationship they had, but there is no doubt they were close.

According to gossip at the nation's capital city, Eleanor developed another romantic attachment, this time with Harry Hopkins, a New Deal administrator. She was also close with her bodyguard, Earl Miller although, again, there is debate about how far the relationship went.

The bottom line is that Eleanor was a kind and loving person. Perhaps she was a bit playful, trying to recapture the feelings she had when spending time with her father. With Franklin, she developed a more maternal approach after his affair. This would prove useful when he suffered the greatest setback in his life.

Chapter 5

Stand-In for Franklin

Franklin Delano Roosevelt contracted polio in 1921; Eleanor correctly believed that he would never regain his mobility. They were wealthy, so they did not need the relatively small income he would make as a politician. However, that was not their reason for pursuing politics in the first place. Franklin wanted to continue his political career. Even more, Eleanor wanted the best for him and wanted to continue to affect the political process.

Eleanor started by overseeing all his medical care and meeting all his physical needs whenever possible. For the first few days, she was his nurse and caregiver. And, even though his physical capabilities had been drastically reduced, Eleanor understood, when no one else did, that he would not be happy if he did not stay in politics.

Franklin had promised his sons to take them on a European vacation. Eleanor took Franklin's place on the excursion and took them to Europe on her own. She managed their household and played mother and father to their children.

Eleanor also encouraged Franklin to try new treatments. When he went to Warm Springs, Georgia to pursue one of these treatment options, she stayed behind, building a career for herself in reform politics. She worked in leadership roles in The Women's City Club of New York, The Women's Trade Union League, the Women's Division of the New York State Democratic Committee, The League of Women Voters, and the World Peace Movement. She was active in the Democratic National Convention in 1924 and 1928, supporting Al Smith for president.

Eleanor, Nancy Cook, and Marion Dickerman founded Val-Kill Industries, a small furniture-making business that sold colonial-era reproductions. This small business grew to become a 4-story factory that employed jobless women. The group also owned the Todhunter School for Girls in New York City, where Eleanor taught government and history.

Then, she went a step further. She became Franklin's right-hand woman after he became governor of New York. She stood in for him to gather information about conditions at state-run institutions and briefed him on her findings. Later, during Franklin's presidential campaigns, Eleanor made appearances for him when he could not attend important events himself. There was one thing she would not do, however. She never spoke for her husband. In 1932, she voted for FDR's election, only the fourth American president's wife to do so.

Chapter 6

A Different Kind of First Lady

With his wife's help, Franklin Delano Roosevelt became president in 1933. Eleanor Roosevelt became First Lady - a role that had been primarily a social one up to that point in American history. Traditionally, the First Lady would make a home in the White House for her husband and children and play host to various teas, dinners, and balls. She would greet guests and help choose the White House china and silverware, along with menus. However, when it was Eleanor's time to take on the role, she was not content to stay in the background. She had an agenda of her own – to promote social reform in whatever ways she could.

Eleanor had feared taking on the role of First Lady, partly because women in that position in the past had given up activism and the projects they had started before their husbands took office. She did not want to fade into the background but wanted instead to use the visibility the position afforded her to create significant changes for her constituents.

Because she became First Lady during the Great Depression, many in the country welcomed her interest in the plight of the poor and unemployed. Working women appreciated her activism for their cause. In fact, she was the leading supporter of Franklin's choices for women to work in federal positions. She also helped secure scholarships for young students and fellowships for artists and writers through government programs.

Other people during that time opposed what they saw as the First Lady's intrusion into the political scene. World War I was over and women had begun to take on more traditional roles with their husbands' return. These people wanted Eleanor to stick to the traditional wifely duties rather than push her way into matters they thought did not concern her.

Yet, Eleanor had more significant projects on her mind when she arrived at the White House in 1932. She wanted to help institute better working conditions and shorter hours for people in the working class. Her work with unions was a top priority for her.

She conferred with President Roosevelt and his advisors, offered her opinions and help in achieving Franklin's goals as well as her own. Louis Howe continued to coach her on politics and orchestrated her appearances on Franklin's behalf. During her 12 years as First Lady, Eleanor traveled extensively, appearing at labor meetings to let workers know that the White House supported them.

In 1933, just as she was beginning her time at the White House, she met with members of the Bonus Army, a group of disgruntled World War I veterans who had marched on Washington to demand early payment of their benefits. They had protested before FDR took office, but Herbert Hoover had sent in the army rather than addressing the issues from the White House. Eleanor met with the former soldiers in their camp and heard them out. They told her about their concerns as American veterans, and she listened and offered them her support. So, rather than fanning the flames of dissent as Hoover had done, Eleanor calmed everyone down and promote a situation in which the government would work with veterans as a team to help them achieve their goals. Singing army songs with them, Eleanor established a beneficial camaraderie between opposing factions to create a peaceful resolution to the protest.

However, not all of Eleanor's projects were so easily handled. In 1933, she would attempt to start a new community, an unusual task for a woman at that time. With Franklin's wholehearted support, she tackled this venture in true Eleanor Roosevelt style.

Chapter 7

The Arthurdale Project

During Franklin's first term as president and Eleanor's first years as First Lady, she began a major project to help poor workers gain a better foothold in society. The project had many detractors at the time, and historians often point to it as Eleanor Roosevelt's only big failure. However, to Eleanor, the community she helped build was a success and one of her crowning achievements.

The Arthurdale project began when Eleanor heard of an idea to create a community for displaced coal miners. The idea fit well with Eleanor's commitment to helping the working class. The community would provide housing, government services, the means for subsistence farming, light industrial jobs, and hope for workers who were struggling.

After learning of it from Eleanor, Franklin Delano Roosevelt supported the project to the point that he federalized it. The Subsistence Homesteads Division of the Interior Department was placed in charge of it, but Eleanor continued to champion it and contribute to its planning and implementation. More communities were planned for the future.

Construction on the Arthurdale, West Virginia settlement began near the end of 1933. Eleanor worked with the Secretary of the Interior to make sure the houses had indoor plumbing, insulation and were outfitted to support the miners' quests to live lives of more dignity and ease than they had had as coal miners and then in the ranks of the unemployed.

Eleanor was enthusiastic about the project and encouraged those in her social network to supply jobs to the community. She raised funds for the project and used her considerable influence to raise awareness of the need for a government-sponsored settlement. She communicated with the public to let them know that this community would benefit the people directly helped as well as the nation as a whole. She explained that these people would be earning their own way in the world and become contributing members of society rather than a drain on it.

There were several problems with Arthurdale, though. First, the Department of the Interior had underestimated construction costs. Therefore, the budget lacked the resources to go ahead with all phases of the plan. When World War II started, the government neither had the interest nor the budget to keep the project going.

The second problem was that the political atmosphere of the time did not support it. Conservatives pointed to Arthurdale as a socialist endeavor and a threat to American democracy and capitalism. And this at a time when Americans were trying to get back on their feet after the devastation of the Great Depression. A pervading belief gripped the country - a belief that honor was closely tied to one's ability to be self-sufficient. What many failed to understand was that the purpose of Arthurdale was to give the miners a chance to do just that.

Meanwhile, Eleanor took an active role in the community. She attended public events such as dances and graduations. She also contacted GE and convinced them to open there for business.

Eventually, the war sentiment and budgetary concerns caused the government to back out of the project. Private individuals and enterprises bought the lands and buildings, and the community became a traditional American town, but one that survived beyond its government support and even flourished. The former miners now had a place and the means to live dignified lives. The settlement, after all, was a success, if not as a government project, certainly as a thriving community of its own.

Another issue came to Eleanor's attention while she was working on the Arthurdale project. She suggested that African Americans be allowed to settle there. She met such opposition that she espoused civil rights for all from then on.

Chapter 8

Stance on Women's Rights

Eleanor came along before the modern feminist movement arrived. General opinion during the Great Depression, just before and during the time Franklin Delano took office for the first time, was that women's place was in the home, backing up their husbands in all aspects of their lives. So, even though Eleanor did not support the Equal Rights Amendment at any time during her life, she did make significant strides towards equal rights and responsibilities for women, considering the time in which she lived.

Before Franklin became president, though, she was already supporting women's' rights. After World War I, Eleanor joined the League of Women Voters in 1920. This became a meaningful cause for her, as she continued to encourage women to vote throughout her life. She strongly felt that voting was one of the most satisfying acts a woman could engage in. She always wanted to have her say, and she encouraged other women to do the same.

She worked with various groups that also supported equal rights for women. In the International Congress of Working Women, she worked with Rose Scheidermann on issues like a fair minimum wage for women, reasonable working hours, improved working conditions in female-dominated occupations, and child labor laws. Working with women's labor organizations, she lent her support to movement agendas like birth control, women's acceptance into labor unions, and getting a living wage.

In the Women's International League of Peace and Freedom, she learned from Carrie Chapman Catt about the women's movement as they worked toward peace in the world. Molly Dewson, Nancy Cook and Marion Dickermen were mentors to Eleanor as well, helping her to understand the need for women's rights and the methods that could be employed to achieve it.

At the 1924 Democratic National Convention, Eleanor got a taste of how women were treated in the party. Its leaders had asked her to be the chairwoman of the platform committee for that year. Eleanor took the job seriously and got input on what it should include from women's groups across the nation. However, when she presented her ideas, she was told she would have to wait outside while the men discussed the proposals. None of their suggestions were added to the platform.

When her work on the platform was completely disregarded and dismissed by the men, Eleanor became even more determined to secure places for women in the government. Just after Franklin took office in the White House, Eleanor began working on getting women appointed to executive-level positions in the federal government. When her requests fell on deaf ears within the administration, Eleanor went directly to FDR. She also spoke to women at speaking engagements, in radio addresses, and in her writings to encourage them to speak up about their concerns, to vote, and to take an active role in the government whenever possible.

In 1928, she managed a get-out-the-vote campaign that was so successful it eclipsed all other such efforts before hers. She wrote that women needed to play the political game just as men did and become party bosses.

Eleanor wanted the New Deal to help women as much as it helped men, and she worked to ensure that women were included in New Deal projects. When World War II came around, Eleanor rallied women to work in the defense industries, civil defense, and the military. She further lobbied for military positions for women in which they could do more than clerical and janitorial work. She helped set up daycare centers for women in the defense industry.

Eleanor Roosevelt and Molly Dewson organized and lobbied for women delegates to the Democratic Convention in 1936. A total of 219 delegates and 302 alternate delegates were appointed because of Molly's and Eleanor's efforts.

While Eleanor felt that women were inherently different from men in their capabilities and talents, she also saw that these attributes would make them good leaders and peacemakers. She was not a feminist in the current sense of the word, but she worked as hard or harder for women's equality than many women who have been called feminists in more recent times. And, her commitment to equal rights and freedom for all showed up across the board. She was not just interested in her own rights, but cared that all people have their fair share of political support. It was this belief that propelled her into the civil rights movement.

Chapter 9

Civil Rights Activist

After failing to win African Americans the opportunity to participate in Arthurdale, Eleanor wanted to know more about the situation of black people in America. She met with Walter White of the NAACP and a group of African American leaders. By the time the meeting was concluded, Eleanor had a better understanding of how unjustly the government had treated black citizens. Concerned with the situation, Eleanor added this to her top priorities for making the country more aware of and sympathetic to the plights of underserved groups.

Eleanor was enraged by the treatment of blacks in America. She wrote extensively about the problem and lobbied the government directly for changes. She was appalled at the lynchings that took place at that time and worked toward legislation to punish those who took part in them.

When the NAACP held an art exhibit to emphasize the cruelty of the lynchings, Eleanor announced that she would attend. She arrived at the exhibit to support the cause, and the country took notice of her presence there. The Daughters of the American Revolution denied Marion Anderson, a prominent black opera singer, the chance to perform at their Constitution Hall. Eleanor was so incensed by this that she immediately withdrew her membership in the prestigious organization.

Eleanor was committed to fighting for freedom for all social groups. When World War II was going on, she was quick to point out that America treated blacks poorly, just as Nazi Germany discriminated against anyone who was not of the Aryan race. This statement was a bold one for a white woman to make, but she was not afraid to say what was on her mind, as she always did once she became politically active.

Another issue that Eleanor fought hard to overcome was the fact that many suggested that the founding documents of the U.S. did not guarantee rights for African Americans. Not only did Eleanor disagree, but she went so far as to write a powerful statement which argued that democracy fails if it does not treat all residents –

including blacks – as valuable members of society deserving equal rights, in her work, the *Moral Basis of Democracy*.

Southerners often criticized Eleanor for supporting blacks' rights. Many of them spread rumors that servants were forming "Eleanor Clubs" to promote rebellion against employers or that black men would push white women to the ground on "Eleanor Tuesdays." These two rumors seem to be based on nothing but the southerners' fears of racial desegregation and African American rights.

Eleanor also flexed her political muscle in fighting for racial justice in the military. At that time, the only job blacks could do in the Navy was mess hall duty. Eleanor pushed for African Americans to be given a chance to show what they could do in more responsible positions.

She lent her political prowess to advance the cause of integration and promote the government's Tuskegee Airmen's training. She even went on a flight with them to show her support. After President Harry Truman took office, Eleanor encouraged him to desegregate the military, which he ultimately did in large part due to her influence.

Eleanor Roosevelt kept up the fight for civil rights up until the end of her life. In later years, there came a time when she agreed to speak on civil disobedience as a means to further the cause of civil rights for African Americans. The prospect of a former First Lady so publicly joining in the fight for civil rights worried the Ku Klux Klan so much that they put a price on her head. The Secret Service told her not to go. However, she responded in true Eleanor Roosevelt style, carrying a revolver for protection and appearing as promised.

Chapter 10

War Work

Eleanor Roosevelt began helping victims of World War II long before America entered the war. Her initial work was with refugees leaving Nazi Germany. She also encouraged Americans at home to support democratic ideals and be courageous in those uncertain times. When the U.S. entered the war, Eleanor attended to the needs of soldiers.

Early on, Eleanor committed herself to aid refugees of the war. The U.S. Immigration policies at that time included strict quotas; only a certain number of people from each country could immigrate to the U.S. However, with what was happening in Europe at the time, Eleanor and others believed that the U.S. should allow more immigrants to come in from war-torn Germany and other European countries affected by the war.

Eleanor worked with several organizations that were focused on trying to get aid to refugees. These included the U.S. Committee for the Care of European Children, the Emergency Rescue Committee and the Children's Crusade for Children. Eleanor was soon well known for her assistance to refugees, to the extent that people wanting to enter the U.S. would petition her directly. She lobbied on their behalf and made it possible for many of them to live in America.

She worked toward the passage of the Child Refugee Bill. If that bill had passed, 10,000 Jewish children would have been able to enter the U.S. each year for two years. This number would have been in addition to the German quota if Congress had passed it. Even though she did not succeed in getting the bill passed, she still worked getting individuals admitted to the country and continued to speak out against restrictions.

Eleanor was concerned with American morale at home. She had already lived through one world war era and felt that the biggest mistake of World War I was that people united over a common enemy but not around a common idealism. So, she promoted democracy and encouraged U.S. citizens to remain hopeful.

Eleanor supported the idea that women could work in defense industries. She worked towards getting childcare centers and lunch counters at such factories to help integrate women into the industries. She convinced FDR that blacks should have equal rights in the workplace, and so he set up the Fair Employment Practices Commission to stop discrimination within the defense industry.

Franklin wanted Eleanor to hold the position of deputy director of the Office of Civilian Defense. In this capacity, she worked with England's Lady Stella Reading to create the "American Social Defense Organization" document. This organization helped establish the Office of Civilian Defense. However, after receiving harsh criticism for appointments she made, Eleanor decided she could no longer be effective in the role and bowed out.

Eleanor helped soldiers in many ways. For example, she kept up personal correspondences with several soldiers during the war. When they told her about a problem they were having, she used her influence to effect solutions. She visited thousands of soldiers in the U.S., in England, and in the South Pacific. When she returned from a trip, she wrote a report on conditions and sent it to the Red Cross.

One other job Eleanor took on was to help the families of soldiers killed in battle. She had read the letter FDR was sending out to these families and found it cold and impersonal. She rewrote the letter to make it more personal and compassionate.

Eleanor was never completely satisfied with what she accomplished during World War II. Her goals were so lofty that, despite her continued efforts and boundless energy, she could do all she wanted to do. Soon, a more personal challenge would occupy the First Lady.

Chapter 11

A Death, Disillusionment and Recovery

When FDR ran for president in 1944, Eleanor campaigned vigorously for him and encouraged him to take a more active role in his own campaign. Eleanor stayed away from political messages during the campaign and focused on getting out the vote. She knew that her presence on the campaign trail would send enough of a message on its own. FDR was elected and began his fourth term as president in 1945.

In April 1945, Franklin was away at the Little White House, his retreat from the Oval Office, in Warm Springs, Georgia. Eleanor received word that he had died of a massive cerebral hemorrhage on April 12th.

She also heard from reliable sources Lucy Mercer Rutherford, his long-ago mistress, had been with him at the time of his death. Even though Eleanor had demanded that FDR end the relationship with Lucy, and Franklin had agreed, the affair had continued for all those years. To make matters worse, Eleanor learned that her daughter Anna had been aware of the affair all along.

Eleanor was shocked and disillusioned by her husband's infidelity and her daughter's silence on the matter. However, regardless of any agony she might have gone through when she found out, she recovered quickly. In a hurry to leave the White House now that her role of First Lady had ended, Eleanor arranged FDR's funeral, wrote her friends acknowledging their support, had all their possessions and papers packed up, and was all ready to move within a week. After hosing a farewell reception on April 19th, Eleanor went home to Val-Kill.

Eleanor was not alone at this time. The friendships and political alliances she had fostered for herself provided support for her in the days following FDR's death and continued to do so for the rest of her life. There were people she could trust with her most private thoughts and feelings – her sadness, her outrage, and her concerns – as well as people who would back her up in her public activities.

Franklin had left Eleanor with one last job to do for him. She was to see that the Hyde Park residence be turned into a museum. So, Eleanor spent several months cataloging, sorting, and listing his historical documents and belongings. The museum opened one year to the day after his death as the Franklin D. Roosevelt Presidential Library and Museum.

Eleanor then moved to an apartment in Greenwich Village to begin the next phase of her life. She jumped back into her old commitments and continued to shape the destiny of humankind. The new president had just the right position for Eleanor, and she was ready to begin.

Chapter 12

Presidential Potential?

Eleanor Roosevelt was a formidable woman and a skilled politician. By the time FDR died, she had gained world recognition as a leader, not only of women but of America in general. So, although no woman had held the office before, it is not surprising that several of her political allies suggested she run for president after her husband's death.

Pundits of the time speculated on what the former First Lady would do with her time, activism, and seemingly unlimited energy. Several positions were suggested for her, including United States Senator, Secretary of Labor, New York state governor, Secretary of State, and yes, president of the United States.

In many ways, Eleanor would have made a good president. She had experience in both foreign and domestic affairs and had learned much from FDR about the issues a president must deal with and the decisions a leader of America would have to make. She knew the current situation at home and abroad much better than many of her contemporaries. And, she was quite active in the Democratic Party and might have secured the nomination if she had been interested in pursuing it.

However, Eleanor had no desire to hold the top office in the U.S. government. In fact, she was surprised that it was even suggested. She made light of the idea and told friends she would like to retire from public life altogether. Of course, they were not convinced she would ever do so. Moreover, even though Eleanor professed a desire to stay out of politics, she worried that FDR's death would mean the end of her influence.

Could Eleanor Roosevelt have handled the presidency? The answer was plain to those who knew her. She was accustomed to the political process and had learned from the top minds in politics. She knew how to handle a campaign and understood what it took to get legislation passed. She was well aware of the enormous responsibility that came with the job, but she had taken on huge responsibilities before. She had learned to play the political game like a pro. Yet, she retained her compassion for the less fortunate in society. She also had a coherent vision for the country and the world.

Instead of seeking office, as she could have done, Eleanor returned to her duties in the organizations she was already involved in. She still wanted to work towards world peace, human rights, and equal rights for women and minorities. She just wanted to do it as a citizen actively engaged in the democratic process. In short, she wanted to change the world for the better. And, President Truman was about to give her an opportunity to do just that. In December 1945, President Truman appointed Eleanor to a position in a fledgling organization that would ultimately change the course of history. The results were nothing less than monumental.

Chapter 13

United Nations Delegate

In October 1945, the United Nations was formed as a response to the war with Germany, Italy, and Japan. In 1942, twenty-six nations signed its founding document, the U.N. Declaration, saying that they would support each other through the war and beyond. Franklin Roosevelt was among the original leaders setting up the organization, and Eleanor had been interested from the start.

President Truman took over where FDR left off, and spoke at the groundbreaking for its new home, emphasizing the need for nations to work together for the betterment of humankind. Along with improving economic conditions and controlling weapons, one of Truman's primary goals for the organization was to ensure individual rights around the world. A top priority was creating a blueprint for human rights. For this task, he selected Eleanor Roosevelt as a delegate to the United Nations.

Eleanor's first assignment was to the United Nations Social, Humanitarian and Cultural Commission, where she unexpectedly made waves in the discussion about the Cold War. She spoke before the General Assembly about refugees from the Soviet Union who feared going back to Russia because of fear they would suffer because of their political ideals. Eleanor spoke up, saying they were not traitors and should not be treated by the U.S.S.R. as such or forced to go home.

Eleanor became chairperson of the United Nations Commission on Human Rights in 1946. In this position, she helped draft the Universal Declaration of Human Rights, a document that has been used ever since then to protect individuals from persecution by their governments. She helped negotiate between delegates from a wide range of cultural backgrounds to make it possible for them to agree on what constituted natural human rights. She surprised everyone at how politically adept she was and at how well she rallied others to support a cause she believed in so completely.

Eleanor not only helped write the declaration, but she lent it her full support in speaking engagements and in her writings. In her presentation of the document in the General Assembly, she encouraged and inspired the delegates to approve it. The United Nations General Assembly approved the Declaration on December 10th of that year.

Eleanor was an influential delegate, always stating her honest and well-thought-out positions to the U.N. members, regardless of any backlash she might have suffered as a result. She followed her conscience, as always, even to the point of criticizing her friend President Truman about his stance on not giving Jews a homeland in Palestine. Eleanor had supported Jewish causes from early on and was not about to give up at that point.

As long as the issue of a Jewish homeland remained unsettled, Eleanor continued to fight for human rights in other areas as well. She worked to develop good relationships between the world community and emerging nations and supported colonies in their quests to break free from colonial rule. Eleanor remained a delegate in the United Nations for seven years, during which she had a profound effect on its direction.

The U.N. presented Eleanor Roosevelt with the first Human Rights prizes as a posthumous award. Her work at the United Nations was among her most notable achievements. At various points along the way, though, many of her supporters had other ideas of how her expertise could be put to use.

Chapter 14

Eleanor, Harry, and John

Eleanor Roosevelt had a profound effect on many of the nation's leaders, both before and after her time in the White House. Harry Truman and John F. Kennedy enjoyed her friendship and called on her political expertise during their administrations.

When Franklin Delano Roosevelt passed away, Eleanor went to see the new president, Harry Truman. President Truman offered his support and condolences and asked her what he could do for her. Eleanor's response shows both her understanding of the challenges Truman faced and the sense of pragmatism she was so famous for. She turned his question back to him, asking Truman if there was anything she and her colleagues and friends could do to help him, now that he was in such a difficult position.

This marked the beginning of a long and fruitful relationship between the former First Lady and the new President. They corresponded over the years, Eleanor sending letters of appreciation, congratulations, and gifts at various intervals. When Eleanor brought up questions about world affairs in her newspaper column or radio addresses, Harry sent letters explaining what was happening at the time, from the president's perception and knowledge. He sent her missives recounting the horrors of the war as they had been told to him. Eleanor asked him whether she should visit Russia as was suggested to her. The two exchanged these letters in 1945 and continued writing to each other until 1959.

During the time Harry Truman was president, Eleanor acted as his sounding board, his sometime confidant, his advisor, his debate opponent, and his helper. Eleanor, for her part, retained the ability to have a significant influence on presidential policy. She did not always agree with the new president, and she was quick to tell him about her reservations concerning his choices. However, Eleanor and Harry were a formidable team in the face of national and world crisis.

In 1961, Eleanor did not want to support John F. Kennedy for president. She preferred to back Adlai Stevenson. She worked hard on

Stevenson's campaign and was quite disappointed that he did not win the Democratic nomination that year. However, Kennedy was not dissuaded. He understood her value to the Democratic Party and wanted her on his side. He courted her approval, and eventually won it.

After Kennedy gave his Inaugural speech in January 1961, Eleanor wrote him a letter of gratitude. She expressed the feeling of freedom she had experienced while listening to his powerful message and promised to support him as the new leader of the country.

Eleanor later interviewed President Kennedy, asking him for his opinions and plans to promote equal rights for women. The interview was well-received by the public and helped establish a long-term collaboration between Kennedy and Roosevelt. These two presidents both used Eleanor's skill and political prowess in important positions during their administrations. Truman sent her to represent the U.S. at the United Nations. Kennedy appointed her to chair the President's Commission on the Status of Women. These were both positions she cared about deeply and turned out to be just the right vehicles for her indomitable individuality.

Chapter 15

Eleanor and the Media

Eleanor Roosevelt spoke her mind. The media usually listened without invitation, but Eleanor did invite them to press conferences often – 348 times during FDR's presidency. She had one stipulation, however. She refused to allow male reporters into those press events. She held the conferences for the Women's Press Corps.

This demand served two purposes. First, it allowed her to speak directly to the women who helped shape the news. Second, it created a situation in which newspapers were forced to keep on female reporters if they wanted first-hand word of the conferences. And of course, this was one of Eleanor's missions – to promote women taking their place in the larger society.

When Eleanor heard that the Gridiron Club only allowed men at their annual press party, she hosted the same type of event at the White House, but hers was for only the female reporters. Her close personal relationship with reporter Lorena Hickok gave her ample opportunities to learn about the press and how it worked. Lorena helped her understand how to use the media to win people to support her causes. Yet, it was Eleanor who spoke directly with the media and said what was on her mind.

While Eleanor was very amenable to the media's needs, she also used them to her advantage. She explained her humanitarian goals and encouraged listeners to join the effort. She made announcements about the organizations she was a member of to further their causes. And, she raised funds to donate to charity. All in all, it was a successful relationship between Eleanor and the media.

Eleanor also gave radio talks during her time as First Lady. She started in 1932 by signing with Pond's cold cream to do twelve shows. She later contracted with other businesses to keep her program going. Her talks covered subjects that were important to women of the day and impacted life in America for all. Some of the topics included higher education and commentaries on current events.

In 1937, amid criticisms that a First Lady should not be involved with commercial enterprises, Eleanor began doing her show for NBC Radio. She did 13 spots for them that year, and the number increased until she was doing 26 in 1940. The next year, she did a special series of broadcasts that proved to be her most popular and the most notable of her radio addresses. Her primary message in these radio talks was that citizens should support their president in his commitment to helping England in the war. She spoke out against the Japanese internment camps in the U.S. and promoted many of FDR's programs and policies. She also encouraged her listeners to volunteer their time and skills to the war effort.

Later on, Eleanor interviewed some of the most influential leaders in the world. These interviews were filmed for newsreels and later broadcast on TV for the fans of leaders like John F. Kennedy, as well as for her own supporters.

Eleanor and the media did not always agree or get along. She received a great deal of flack from the media, primarily due to her own professional career as a freelance journalist and editor. Yet, her writings inspired a generation of women and remain a national treasure today.

Chapter 16

Speaking Tours and Writings

The Harvard Lampoon ridiculed Eleanor as the editor of the short-lived magazine *Babies, Just Babies* just before FDR took office. While Eleanor thought of the magazine as an opportunity to help educate women, the media did not seem to understand her aims. Even the Women's National Press Club made fun of the magazine.

Overall, though, her relationship with the media was a mutually beneficial one, and one she built throughout her time in the public eye. Her writings and radio addresses not only put Eleanor on the media's radar, but they also endeared her to the American public.

Immediately before FDR took office as president, Eleanor wrote an editorial for *Women's Daily News* that argued against his public spending policies. This prompted the president-elect to respond to her editorial in the next issue of the magazine. Then, just after he took office, she started writing a monthly column for *Woman's Home Companion*. In the column, she answered readers' questions and commented on the positions they took on a wide range of issues.

When FDR was campaigning for his second term as president, Eleanor stopped writing for the Woman's Home Companion. However, her writing did not stop there. She continued to write articles, publishing over 60 of them while she was First Lady.

Eleanor was also a prolific author, writing and publishing more books while she was First Lady than anyone who held that position had ever done before. Her overall style nurtured people to take an active part in the political process, live their lives with dignity, and contribute to society as a whole. She wrote about world affairs with the same expertise as she wrote about her own life in her autobiography. She wrote both nonfiction and fiction.

Eleanor had a successful career as a speaker and lecturer, too. She wrote outlines for all her 1400 speeches and then rounded them out when she took the podium. At first, her speeches seemed stiff and formal. Many found her voice irritating. So, she worked with a voice coach and honed her messages to become a better and more influential public speaker. In 1935, Eleanor began a contract to deliver two lecture tours per year. As a paid speaker, she gave about 700 speeches before the contract concluded in 1941.

Eleanor's speeches were often about life in the White House, but she also presented serious topics regarding issues that were important to the nation as a whole. The audiences for the speeches were usually large, but some varied from relatively small groups to groups of over 15,000 listeners.

In her final years, Eleanor Roosevelt continued to speak to all who would listen about the causes she believed were just. After the Freedom Riders faced racial injustice, Eleanor again spoke out. This time, she wanted to encourage people to fight for civil rights and even demanded that news outlets cover civil rights stories. And, after 40 years of standing against it, she finally supported women's fight to have an Equal Rights Amendment. Eleanor never stopped speaking, but she also never stopped learning. Her life was a model for genuine engagement with the world.

Chapter 17

Honors to an American Icon

On November 7, 1962, at the age of 78 years, Eleanor Roosevelt died of heart failure due to bone marrow tuberculosis. President John F. Kennedy ordered all U.S. flags to be flown at half-mast in honor of her memory. Many prominent leaders, including Kennedy, Eisenhower and Adlai Stevenson, as well as the personal friends she had made during her public life joined her family at her funeral.

The Eleanor Roosevelt National Historic Site at her home in Val-Kill was set aside in 1977. In 1996, the Eleanor Roosevelt Monument was placed in Riverside Park, New York.

Although Eleanor regretted missing the opportunity to get a college education, people around the world eventually recognized that it was only the certificate that was lacking. She had learned more than she might have learned at any university. Thus, Alpha Kappa Alpha sorority made her an honorary member. And, numerous colleges gave her a total of 48 honorary degrees during her lifetime.

She won the United Nations Human Rights Prize posthumously. Two of the subsistence communities she fought for are named for her. Her books tell her story and the story of the nation at the time in which she lived. She was also nominated for a Nobel Peace Prize after her death, but the nomination had little hope of success since this prize has never been awarded posthumously or even considered after the person's death.

Many people who heard Eleanor speak are still alive to tell the story. When they are gone, her memory will live on in the organizations, writings, and recordings that kept her busy during her life. And, people who read historians' accounts of her words and deeds will continue to honor her for the national treasure that she was.

Eleanor Roosevelt was truly a unique and powerful individual. She has become an American icon of sensibility, tenaciousness, and reason. Her efforts for world peace have helped the nations protect themselves and each other.

The world would be different without the life of this amazing woman.

Conclusion

Eleanor Roosevelt was a different kind of woman than had ever graced the position of First Lady before and will never be replaced. People of her time knew her passion for the causes she supported. They understood that she was far more than an appendage to the office of the presidency. She gave people a chance to know her for who she was and call on her for help in times of crisis.

Yet, in recent years, Eleanor Roosevelt has been misunderstood by many who never had the opportunity to meet her. To a contemporary world, Eleanor Roosevelt may seem bland or even unimportant. That is a shame, for she taught the world how to stand up for its rights, and for that, the world should be forever grateful.

Printed in Great Britain
by Amazon

40649891R00040